FINDING A VOICE:
Women's Fight for Equality in U.S. Society

SEEKING THE RIGHT TO VOTE

LEEANNE GELLETLY

FINDING A VOICE:
Women's Fight for Equality in U.S. Society

TITLES IN THIS SERIES

A WOMAN'S PLACE IN EARLY AMERICA

ORIGINS OF THE WOMEN'S RIGHTS MOVEMENT

SEEKING THE RIGHT TO VOTE

WOMEN'S RIGHTS ON THE FRONTIER

THE EQUAL RIGHTS AMENDMENT

WOMEN GO TO WORK, 1941–45

WOMEN IN THE CIVIL RIGHTS MOVEMENT

THE WOMEN'S LIBERATION MOVEMENT, 1960–1990

THE FEMINIST MOVEMENT TODAY

SEEKING THE RIGHT TO VOTE

LEEANNE GELLETLY

MASON CREST
PHILADELPHIA

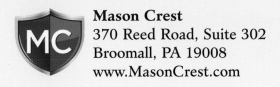

Mason Crest
370 Reed Road, Suite 302
Broomall, PA 19008
www.MasonCrest.com

CPSIA Compliance Information: Batch #FF2012-3. For further information, contact Mason Crest at 1-866-MCP-Book.

First printing
1 3 5 7 9 8 6 4 2

Library of Congress Cataloging-in-Publication Data

Gelletly, LeeAnne.
  Seeking the right to vote / LeeAnne Gelletly.
      p. cm. — (Finding a voice : women's fight for equality in U.S. society)
  Includes bibliographical references and index.
   ISBN 978-1-4222-2354-3 (hardcover)
   ISBN 978-1-4222-2364-2 (pbk.)
  1. Women—Suffrage—United States—History—Juvenile literature. I. Title.
  JK1898.G45 2012
  324.6'230973—dc23
                                        2011043487

Publisher's note: All quotations in this book are taken from original sources, and contain the spelling and grammatical inconsistencies of the original texts.

Picture credits: Library of Congress: 3, 12, 16, 19, 20, 21, 23, 24, 25, 26, 27, 28, 30, 31, 32, 33, 34, 35, 36, 38, 40, 41, 42, 43, 45, 46, 49, 51, 52, 55; National Archives: 50; Wikimeda Commons: 8, 14.

TABLE OF CONTENTS

INTRODUCTION

A. Page Harrington, director, Sewall-Belmont House & Museum

As the Executive Director of the Sewall-Belmont House & Museum, which is the fifth and final headquarters of the historic National Woman's Party (NWP), I am surrounded each day by artifacts that give voice to the stories of Alice Paul, Lucy Burns, Doris Stevens, Alva Belmont, and the whole community of women who waged an intense campaign for the right to vote during the second decade of the 20th century. The original photographs, documents, protest banners, and magnificent floor-length capes worn by these courageous activists during marches and demonstrations help us bring their work to life for the many groups who tour the museum each week.

The perseverance of the suffragists bore fruit in 1920, with the ratification of the 19th Amendment. It was a huge milestone, though certainly not the end of the journey toward full equality for American women.

Throughout much (if not most) of American history, social conventions and the law constrained female participation in the political, economic, and intellectual life of the nation. Women's voices were routinely stifled, their contributions downplayed or dismissed, their potential ignored. Underpinning this state of affairs was a widely held assumption of male superiority in most spheres of human endeavor.

Always, however, there were women who gave the lie to gender-based stereotypes. Some helped set the national agenda. For example, in the years preceding the Revolutionary War, Mercy Otis Warren made a compelling case for American independence through her writings. Abigail Adams, every bit the intellectual equal of her husband, counseled John Adams to "remember the ladies and be more generous and favorable to them than your ancestors" when creating laws for the new country. Sojourner Truth helped lead the movement to abolish slavery in the 19th century. A hundred years later, Rosa Parks galvanized the civil rights movement, which finally secured for African Americans the promise of equality under the law.

The lives of these women are familiar today. So, too, are the stories of groundbreakers such as astronaut Sally Ride; Supreme Court justice Sandra Day O'Connor; and Nancy Pelosi, Speaker of the House of Representatives.

But famous figures are only part of the story. The path toward gender equality was also paved—and American society shaped—by countless women whose individual lives and deeds have never been chronicled in depth. These include the women who toiled alongside their fathers and brothers and husbands on the western frontier; the women who kept U.S. factories running during World War II; and the women who worked tirelessly to promote the goals of the modern feminist movement.

The FINDING A VOICE series tells the stories of famous and anonymous women alike. Together these volumes provide a wide-ranging overview of American women's long quest to achieve full equality with men—a quest that continues today.

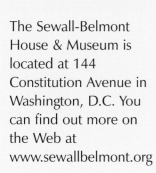

The Sewall-Belmont House & Museum is located at 144 Constitution Avenue in Washington, D.C. You can find out more on the Web at www.sewallbelmont.org

This sidewalk plaque in Rochester, New York, marks the spot where Susan B. Anthony cast a ballot in the 1872 presidential election. For this action she was arrested and placed on trial at the Ontario County Courthouse in nearby Canandaigua, New York.

1

"I HOPE YOU VOTED, TOO"

"Well I have been & gone & done it!!—positively voted the Republican ticket—strait this a.m. at 7 Oclock—& swore my vote in at that . . . for five days I have been on the constant run—but to splendid purpose—So all right—I hope you voted too."

Susan B. Anthony wrote these words on November 5, 1872. She was sharing good news with her friend Elizabeth Cady Stanton. Anthony had cast a ballot for Ulysses S. Grant for president. She had voted. And in 1872 America that was something women were not allowed to do.

WITHOUT "A LAWFUL RIGHT"

Anthony believed women should be allowed to vote. And she had been working since 1852 for that right. She gave speeches. And she lobbied lawmakers. Finally she decided to try to register to vote. She figured she would be turned away. Then she would sue in court. A favorable court decision would give all women the vote.

But Anthony was surprised. She convinced officials to allow her to register in Rochester, New York. Her three sisters also registered. Four days later the women voted in the presidential election.

Soon after, Anthony was arrested. So were other suffragists who voted

FAST FACT

Suffrage refers to the right to vote. Most women seeking the vote called themselves *suffragists*. People who opposed suffrage for women used the more insulting term *suffragettes*. Later, both terms were common.

that day. They were charged with "knowingly voting without having a lawful right to vote." Anthony was released on bail. And a trial was set for the following June.

SENECA FALLS CONVENTION

Susan B. Anthony was not the first to demand votes for women. Reformers Elizabeth Cady Stanton and Lucretia Mott helped start that campaign in 1848. They called a convention to discuss women's rights.

Stanton and Mott believed that society and laws had to change. Women deserved to be treated as equals. At the time, women had few rights. Most colleges refused to accept them. This excluded them from many professions. They could not become doctors, ministers, or lawyers. By law, married women were the property of their husbands. And women also had no political rights. They could not vote in elections. They could not hold public office. And they could not serve on juries.

On July 19 and 20, 1848, several hundred men and women met in Seneca Falls, New York. Many of them worked in reform movements. A large number were abolitionists—people committed to ending slavery. Women abolitionists were familiar with being excluded. Because they were women, they had been barred from speaking at meetings. They had been prevented from working for their cause. And they had had enough.

At the convention Stanton presented a "Declaration of Sentiments." She had written the document. It noted the women's complaints. And it listed 11 goals that would help women achieve equality to men. One of the goals stated,

> it is the duty of the women of this country to secure to themselves their sacred right to the elective franchise.

The *elective franchise* refers to the right to vote. In mid-19th century America it was unheard of for a woman to want to vote. So the goal was controversial. But at the end of the convention, 100 men and women signed the declaration. For the first time women in the United States publicly demanded the right to vote.

WORKING FOR THE VOTE

The Seneca Falls Convention inspired a movement. Many women joined the effort to gain "woman suffrage." From their work in reform movements, they knew what to do. They organized and publicized conventions. They lectured as platform speakers. They circulated petitions. And they lobbied politicians.

Stanton believed women needed a voice in government. As voters they could influence laws. And new laws could change women's unfair treatment. In a September 1848 speech, she wrote, "The right is ours. Have it we must—use it we will."

In the early 1850s Stanton met Anthony. They quickly became good friends. And they formed a working partnership. Both felt strongly about

FAST FACT

In 1866 Elizabeth Cady Stanton became the first woman to run for election to the U.S. House of Representatives. As an Independent from New York, she received 24 votes of 12,000.

women's rights. Together they organized petition campaigns. Stanton wrote articles, letters, and speeches. Anthony organized lectures and delivered many of Stanton's speeches.

But in 1861 the U.S. Civil War began. Suffrage workers agreed to stop agitating for the vote. Women turned their attention to helping with the war effort.

SUSAN B. ANTHONY (1820–1906)

Susan Brownell Anthony was born on February 15, 1820, near Adams, Massachusetts. Her family later moved to Rochester, New York. She was raised in a Quaker family. Quakers believe that men and women are equal before God. So she grew up believing in the equality of men and women.

Anthony first worked as a schoolteacher. She later became a social reformer. She worked to end slavery. And she supported temperance reform. (*Temperance* refers to limiting the use of alcoholic beverages.) But she devoted her life to women's suffrage.

In partnership with Elizabeth Cady Stanton, Anthony worked for women's rights. She gave speeches. She organized petition campaigns and demonstrations. And she lobbied state and national legislators.

To obtain the vote, Anthony founded several organizations. In 1866 she helped found the American Equal Rights Association. In 1869 she cofounded the National Woman Suffrage Association. Later she served as president of the National American Woman Suffrage Association.

Anthony also trained women to follow in her footsteps. She called these younger suffragists her "nieces." They affectionately referred to her as "Aunt Susan." Anthony's "nieces" would help ensure passage of the amendment that granted suffrage for women. It was known as the Susan B. Anthony Amendment.

UNIVERSAL SUFFRAGE

The war ended in 1865. That year the U.S. Congress passed the Thirteenth Amendment. It abolished slavery. Congress next considered voting rights. Suffragists renewed the call for the vote. But the Fourteenth Amendment protected citizenship rights only for black Americans. It defined citizens as "all persons born or naturalized in the United States." It guaranteed equal protection under the law. And it also specified that voters were "male."

Stanton and Anthony lobbied to change the amendment. They wanted to remove the word *male*. All people, they argued, deserved the vote. They wanted the amendment to allow universal suffrage. That is, they wanted the vote for men and women, blacks and whites. Stanton and Anthony held a petition drive. They gathered 10,000 signatures on a petition that demanded universal suffrage. In January 1866, they presented it to Congress.

Stanton and Anthony also founded an organization that promoted universal suffrage. The American Equal Rights Association (AERA) had many members. But their lobbying did not work. Legislators did not change the Fourteenth Amendment. And in June 1866 it was passed by Congress. By 1868 it would be ratified. (To become part of the U.S. Constitution, an amendment must be officially approved, or *ratified*. Three-fourths of the state legislatures must ratify a federal amendment.)

Next, Congress debated another amendment. The Fifteenth Amendment stated that citizens could not be denied the right to vote on the basis of race. It made no mention of gender. Some AERA members supported the amendment. Susan B. Anthony and Elizabeth Cady Stanton opposed it. It did not provide universal suffrage.

In 1868 Congress passed the Fifteenth Amendment. It was ratified in 1870. This meant that black men were guaranteed the right to vote. Women were not. The drive for woman suffrage had failed.

RIGHT OF CITIZENSHIP

Two years later Anthony was arrested for voting. After being released on bail, she defended her right to vote. She gave a series of speeches. She had

In 1871 Victoria Claflin Woodhull (1838–1927) spoke before the Judiciary Committee of the U.S. House of Representatives. She argued that the Fourteenth and Fifteenth Amendments, which granted U.S. citizens the right to vote, should apply to both women and men. Susan B. Anthony attempted to use this argument to justify the legality of her vote in the 1872 election.

been born in the United States. So she was a U.S. citizen. The Fourteenth Amendment said so. "[I]n . . . voting, I not only committed no crime," she insisted, "but, instead, simply exercised my citizen's rights, guaranteed to me and all United States citizens by the National Constitution."

Anthony's case came to trial in June 1873. But the judge would not let Anthony testify. He had already written his opinion. And he directed the jury to find her guilty. It did. But she refused to pay the $100 fine.

DEVOTED TO THE CAUSE

Anthony would spend her life seeking the vote for women. She would live to see women attain suffrage in a few western states. But she would not be alive when a federal women's suffrage amendment became part of the U.S. Constitution.

Yet, Anthony had confidence that it would happen one day. With the support of so many women who were "true and devoted to the cause," the vote would come. "With such women consecrating their lives," she would later say, "failure is impossible!"

2

DIVIDED EFFORTS

When Susan B. Anthony tried to vote in 1872, there were two separate groups working for women's rights. Disagreement over the Fifteenth Amendment had split the movement. Two separate groups had emerged in 1869.

Anthony and Elizabeth Cady Stanton founded the National Woman Suffrage Association (NWSA). Abolitionist Lucy Stone helped found the American Woman Suffrage Association (AWSA). Both groups worked for women's suffrage. But they no longer worked together.

NATIONAL WOMAN SUFFRAGE ASSOCIATION

Stanton served as president of the NWSA. Anthony was vice-president. Based in New York City, the group worked for various issues affecting women. But of most importance was the vote.

Anthony and Stanton had a reputation for being extreme. Their organization was also considered radical. And their newspaper reflected this philosophy. It was named the *Revolution*. Its motto proclaimed, "Men, their rights and nothing more; women, their rights and nothing less!" The NWSA initially did not allow men to join.

Although women could not legally vote, some NWSA suffragists made

ELIZABETH CADY STANTON (1815–1902)

Elizabeth Cady was born on November 12, 1815, in Johnstown, New York. She grew up in a wealthy family. Her father, Daniel Cady, was a judge. Elizabeth had an advanced education for a woman at the time. She attended Troy Female Seminary. And she studied law, using books in her father's office.

After graduating, Elizabeth became involved in the antislavery movement. In 1840 she married abolitionist Henry Stanton. In 1848 she helped organize the first women's rights convention. It was held in Seneca Falls, New York.

In partnership with Susan B. Anthony, Stanton worked for various causes. The two women campaigned to change laws. They gave lectures on women's rights. And they worked to win the vote for women. With Anthony, Stanton founded the National Woman Suffrage Association. She also served as the first president of the National American Woman Suffrage Association.

Stanton helped write and edit a history of the suffrage movement. She also wrote *The Woman's Bible* and an autobiography, *Eighty Years and More*. She died in October 1902 in New York City.

the attempt. During the early 1870s members in at least 10 different states tried to register to vote. Like Anthony, they claimed the right of citizenship. They pointed to the Fourteenth Amendment. They were born in the United States. So they were citizens. But few women managed to even register. Most were turned away.

In Missouri an official named Reese Happersett refused to let Virginia Louisa Minor register. She sued. In 1875 the case of *Minor v. Happersett* reached the U.S. Supreme Court. The Court ruled against Minor. The judges said that the Constitution did not guarantee women the right to vote in federal elections. Voting requirements were set by the states. And the states had the right to prohibit women from voting.

"DECLARATION OF RIGHTS"

The following year the NWSA held a demonstration. On July 4, 1876, the nation was celebrating its 100-year anniversary. At a Centennial program in Philadelphia, Anthony disrupted the ceremonies. She stood in front of the Liberty Bell. And she read aloud from the "Declaration of Rights for Women." It had been written by Stanton and Matilda Joslyn Gage.

The U.S. government gave all men "the full rights of citizenship," Anthony proclaimed. At the same time, "all women still suffer the degradation of disfranchisement." She added:

> We ask . . . no special favors, no special privileges, no special legislation. We ask justice, we ask equality, we ask that all the civil and political rights that belong to citizens of the United States, be guaranteed to us and our daughters forever.

THE SIXTEENTH AMENDMENT

Court rulings did not work. Demonstrations were not successful. So NWSA leaders decided to try to obtain the vote through a federal amendment. Stanton and Anthony wrote the text. Its wording was similar to the text of the Fifteenth Amendment. It said:

> The right of citizens of the United States to vote shall not be denied or abridged by the United States or by any State on account of sex. Congress shall have power to enforce this article by appropriate legislation.

FAST FACT

Matilda Joslyn Gage (1826–1898) worked closely with Susan B. Anthony and Elizabeth Cady Stanton. She helped organize suffrage campaigns. She also lectured and wrote for NWSA newspapers.

In January 1878 Senator Aaron A. Sargent introduced the amendment in Congress. But the Senate did not vote on it. Nine years passed. Finally, in January 1887, the Senate held a vote. But only 16 of 76 senators voted in favor. The proposed 16th Amendment was defeated.

In the years that followed, the amendment would be introduced each time Congress met. Suffragists would lobby for its passage. But hearings were seldom held. The suffrage amendment was not brought to a vote.

THE LYCEUM CIRCUIT

Anthony and Stanton worked to spread the word about the NWSA and women's rights. During the 1870s and early 1880s, they were paid speakers on the lyceum circuit. (A *lyceum* is a lecture hall. Speaker's bureaus would sign up talented lecturers who went on tours, or circuits.)

Anthony and Stanton became lyceum favorites. They talked with humor and authority on women's issues. And they called for a woman's right to vote. A major goal was to educate women. Many women did not believe they deserved the vote. The two activists worked to change their minds.

The NWSA leaders spent many years on the road. They traveled throughout the nation. Stanton would later write of Anthony,

> There is scarce a town, however small, from New York to San Francisco, that has not heard her ringing voice. Who can number the speeches she has made on lyceum platforms, in churches, schoolhouses, halls, barns, and in the open air, with a lumber wagon or a cart for her rostrum?

THE AMERICAN WOMAN SUFFRAGE ASSOCIATION

Lyceum speakers also came from the AWSA. Based in Boston, it was more moderate than the NWSA. And it was larger. It had more members because it allowed men to be members. They even served as officers. The first AWSA president was a man named Henry Ward Beecher. Lucy Stone headed the executive committee.

Alice Stone Blackwell (1857–1950) holds a copy of the *Women's Journal*, the influential newspaper her parents Lucy Stone and Henry Blackwell had founded and edited from 1870 to 1872. Alice Stone Blackwell would take over as editor-in-chief in 1883; she maintained that position for more than 30 years. In 1930 she published a biography of her mother.

Stone also served as editor of the AWSA newspaper. It was called the *Woman's Journal*. Other editors included Henry Blackwell and lyceum speaker Mary Livermore. The *Woman's Journal* began publication in January 1870. It would be printed for 47 years. It would become known as the "voice of the woman's movement."

STATE SUFFRAGE CAMPAIGNS

The AWSA worked for state suffrage. Volunteers organized petition drives and presented petitions to state legislatures. They lobbied state lawmakers and delegates to constitutional conventions. They asked that the word *male* be removed from state constitutions. And they asked legislatures to hold state referendums.

A *referendum* is a general vote by the electorate on a single political question. In this case the question was whether to let women vote. The *electorate* refers to qualified voters. State laws allowed only men to vote. So

In 1879 attorney Belva Lockwood (1830–1917) became the first woman to practice law before the U.S. Supreme Court. She founded the National Equal Rights Party. In 1884 and 1888, she ran for U.S. president.

when women's suffrage appeared on the ballot, the AWSA organized campaigns. Lecturers gave speeches. Volunteers printed and handed out thousands of leaflets. And they canvassed door to door. Suffragists worked to convince the male electorate to give women the vote.

WOMAN'S CHRISTIAN TEMPERANCE UNION

Suffrage campaign efforts received help from the Woman's Christian Temperance Union (WCTU). This reform organization worked to help women in families with alcoholics. It was led by Frances Willard.

A goal of the WCTU was to outlaw alcohol. Willard believed that if women had the vote, they would vote to prohibit the sale of alcohol. So her organization allied with both the NWSA and the AWSA. As a result, hundreds of thousands of WCTU members participated in suffrage campaigns.

Liquor and brewing companies became bitter enemies of women's

FAST FACT

Before they won the vote, suffragists would wage 56 referendum campaigns. They would take place in 29 different states and territories.

suffrage. They knew prohibition laws would put their companies out of business. So they poured money into campaigns that worked against allowing women the vote.

THE WEST

By 1870 there were two places where women had the vote. Both were in the west. In 1869 the legislature of Wyoming Territory gave women the vote. Utah Territory followed suit in 1870.

But it took another two decades before a state granted suffrage. During that time numerous referendums were held. In some states the suffrage question appeared on ballots several times. But each time the electorate voted against it. To make matters worse, in 1887 Utah women were disenfranchised by an act of Congress.

The first state to give women the vote would be a new one. In 1890 Wyoming Territory joined the Union. Its state constitution guaranteed women the vote.

This illustration from the November 24, 1888, issue of *Frank Leslie's Illustrated Newspaper* depicts women voting in Cheyenne, Wyoming. When this article appeared the territory was preparing to apply for statehood, and the idea of a state where women could vote seemed unusual to many Americans.

3

THE MOVEMENT REUNITES

In the late 1880s NWSA and AWSA leaders began talks. They decided to unite the two groups. The daughter of Lucy Stone, Alice Stone Blackwell, helped negotiate the merger.

THE NATIONAL AMERICAN WOMAN SUFFRAGE ASSOCIATION

The result was the National American Woman Suffrage Association. Known as NAWSA, it formed in 1890. Elizabeth Cady Stanton served as president. Lucy Stone headed the executive committee. In 1892, Susan B. Anthony replaced Stanton as president.

NAWSA pushed for the vote at the state level. The goal was to win the vote one state at a time. A state that gave women full voting rights was known as a suffrage state. It was hoped that as the number of suffrage states increased, so would support for a federal amendment.

ORGANIZERS

Carrie Chapman Catt was one of NAWSA's younger members. She pushed for a new direction. She noted, "The chief work of suffragists for the past forty years has been education and agitation, and not organization." This lack of organization was a problem. NAWSA had many branches. Groups were working at the national, state, and local levels. Their work needed to be coordinated.

In addition Catt believed that NAWSA needed to establish a permanent presence in every state. She called for full-time, paid workers. These "organizers" would be trained to set up local suffrage groups. With local organizations in place, NAWSA could better direct suffrage campaigns.

As chair of NAWSA's Organization Committee, Catt helped establish clubs in every state and territory. The Committee held public meetings. And it raised funds. Membership in NAWSA grew. In 1893 there were 13,000 members. By 1910 there were 75,000.

LUCY STONE (1818–1893)

Lucy Stone was born August 13, 1818, near West Brookfield, Massachusetts. In 1847 she graduated from Oberlin College. Later she became an anti-slavery lecturer. But at the time people did not approve of women speaking publicly. Stone was often condemned. That treatment inspired her to work for equal rights for women.

Stone helped organize the first national women's rights convention. It was held in 1850 in Worcester, Massachusetts. Five years later Lucy married abolitionist Henry Blackwell. But she did not take his name. She became the first American woman to keep her maiden name after marriage.

After the death of her second child in 1859, Stone withdrew from public speaking. But she returned a decade later. She became a leader in the women's rights movement. In 1869 she helped found the American Woman's Suffrage Association. She also founded its newspaper, the *Woman's Journal*.

Stone served as an officer for the National American Woman Suffrage Association. She remained active in NAWSA until her death in October 1893.

CARRIE CHAPMAN CATT (1859–1947)

Carrie Lane was born January 9, 1859, in Ripon, Wisconsin. She grew up in Iowa. After graduating from Iowa State College in 1880, she became a high school principal. Within two years, she was school superintendent.

Carrie married Leo Chapman and moved to San Francisco. There she worked as a newspaper reporter. After her husband died, she returned to Iowa. She became active in state suffrage work for NAWSA.

In 1890 Carrie married again. Her husband George Catt strongly supported Carrie's suffrage work. She was a talented public speaker. And she soon rose to a leadership position with the National American Woman Suffrage Association. In 1900 she succeeded Susan B. Anthony as president.

After her husband's death in 1905, Catt turned to promoting suffrage around the world. She served as president of the International Woman Suffrage Alliance. In 1915 she helped found the Woman's Peace Party.

That year Catt was reelected as president of NAWSA. She was an effective political strategist and fundraiser. Her efforts promoted the passage of a constitutional amendment giving women the right to vote. She also helped ensure its ratification.

FOUR STATES

NAWSA suffragists lobbied their legislators. They asked for referendums. They requested changes to state constitutions. And they campaigned during elections to pass referendums.

There were some successes. In 1893 male voters in Colorado became the first state to pass a referendum granting suffrage. In 1896 Utah became a state and re-instituted the vote for women. That same year an Idaho referendum passed. But there were also failures. In New York, women obtained 600,000 signatures on petitions. But state legislators refused to place a suffrage referendum on the ballot.

By 1896 women had the right to vote in four states. They were Wyoming, Utah, Colorado, and Idaho. But then the victories stopped.

EXCLUDED BY RACE

The suffrage movement had evolved from the antislavery movement. But during the 1880s and 1890s, black women found themselves excluded from NAWSA.

Most members were white and middle class. In the South, NAWSA state and local branches did not allow blacks to join. These groups wanted the vote for white women only. The national leaders of NAWSA did not object. They did not want to lose the support of white southern women.

Mary Church Terrell tried to work in NAWSA. She called for opportunities for black women. In an 1896 speech before NAWSA members, she spoke for all African American women. "Seeking no favors because of our color, nor patronage because of our needs," she said, "we knock at the bar of justice, asking an equal chance."

But opportunities for black women to participate were few. Many decided to form separate organizations to deal with racial inequality. Some of these groups also worked for suffrage. In 1896 many of these clubs united. They formed the National Association of Colored Women (NACW). Mary Church Terrell served as the first president of the NACW.

Mary Church Terrell (1863–1954) was the daughter of former slaves. She graduated from Oberlin College in 1884, becoming one of the first African-American women to earn a college degree. Terrell worked with both Frederick Douglass and Booker T. Washington on campaigns promoting civil rights for African Americans, as well as being very active in the women's suffrage movement.

A delegate's ribbon from the National American Women Suffrage Association annual convention.

A TRADITIONAL APPROACH

Meanwhile NAWSA focused on making the idea of women's suffrage acceptable to traditionalists. NAWSA postcards, cartoons, and fliers showed images of women as mothers and homemakers. Suffragists reminded readers that a woman's place was in the home. But her family concerns included the community. And that great community included the state and nation. One writer explained, "[T]he State is but the larger family, the nation the old homestead," she wrote. And "in this national home there is a room . . . and a duty for 'mother.'" That duty was the responsibility of a woman to vote.

Women were also portrayed as moral leaders. They were praised as having the morals to fix social problems. Their vote would "clean up" corrupt politics. Through their "social housekeeping," women would fix the nation's problems.

SOCIAL REFORMERS

And by the 1890s, many women were fixing the country's problems. A large number of them were college-educated social workers. Women could now choose from dozens of colleges. Some were only for women. Vassar opened its doors in 1865. Wellesley and Smith Colleges were founded in 1875. Other schools were coeducational. They included Oberlin, which opened to women in 1837, and Swarthmore, founded in 1864.

Female college graduates were working for social change. They saw the problems of rapidly growing U.S. cities. There was great poverty. There

During the 19th century Jane Addams (left) and other reformers wanted to improve the lives of American families by providing better schools and eliminating the exploitation of children by factory owners. (Right) Young workers in a Tennessee textile mill, circa 1910.

was substandard housing. Many low-income residents were immigrants who did not speak English. In 1889 Jane Addams and Ellen Gates Starr founded Hull House in Chicago. This was the first settlement house. Settlement houses were community centers established in city slums. They offered services to improve the lives of the poor. Hull House offered education, day care, and medical care. By 1890, more than 100 settlement

FAST FACT

Changes in attitudes toward suffrage came as more women worked. In 1890 4 million women held jobs outside the home. By 1910 that number had doubled to 8 million.

Anna Howard Shaw (1847–1919) served as NAWSA president from 1904 to 1915. During the First World War, Shaw chaired the women's committee of the Council of National Defense. She later became the first woman to receive the Distinguished Service Medal.

houses had been founded across the United States. Most were established by women.

Women reformers addressed problems caused by poverty. They also worked to do away with child labor. The practice of using children workers was common in the textile industry. Many women came to believe that government laws were needed to fix society's ills. And to influence legislation women needed the vote. Support for women's suffrage continued to grow.

NEW LEADERSHIP

The early leaders of the suffrage movement were growing old. Lucy Stone died in 1893. Elizabeth Cady Stanton passed away in 1902. Her good friend Susan B. Anthony lived four years longer. She died in 1906.

Anthony had stepped down as NAWSA president in 1900. Carrie Chapman Catt took her place. But Catt left the presidency after just a few years. She resigned in 1904, when her husband became gravely ill. He died the following year. Afterward Catt worked with the International Woman Suffrage Alliance. She had helped found the group in 1902. Women in countries such as England, Poland, Germany, France, and Bulgaria were trying to win the vote. As president of the Alliance, Catt gave speeches throughout Europe.

Anna Howard Shaw assumed the presidency of NAWSA. She had been a national speaker for the organization since the late 1880s. And she had served since 1900 as vice-president. Shaw was a committed activist. She was also a physician and the first ordained female Methodist minister in the United States. During her tenure, the number of states with full suffrage would grow to 11.

4

A RENEWED PURPOSE

During the early 1900s the face of the movement changed. Suffragists were no longer from only the rich and middle classes. There were also factory workers and other working-class women. They wanted better wages and working conditions for women. And they wanted the vote.

In New York City Elizabeth Cady Stanton's daughter brought together women from all classes. Harriot Stanton Blatch founded a group in 1907 called the Equality League of Self-Supporting Women. It later became the Women's Political Union (WPU). The WPU organized the first major suffrage march.

"VOTES FOR WOMEN"

Blatch had lived in England. She worked with British women who were trying to win the right to vote. To raise public awareness British suffragists held parades and open-air meetings. Blatch wanted to call attention to women's suffrage in the United States. So she used the same tactics. Her group organized a large-scale parade.

The parade took place in May 1910 in New York City. Several thousand women marched. Most were dressed in white. White, they said, represented the purity of their cause. The suffragists marched down Fifth Avenue. Their signs and banners demanded "Votes for Women."

Harriot Stanton Blatch (standing) speaks to a crowd of men on Wall Street, circa 1910. Blatch (1856–1940), the daughter of Elizabeth Cady Stanton, helped bring working-class women into the suffrage movement.

The parades became an annual event in New York City. Each year, the numbers of marchers grew. In May 1911 about 3,000 supporters marched. In May 1912 the numbers swelled to 20,000. Suffrage parades were soon being held in cities across the nation. They provided good publicity. Newspaper reports kept the issue in the public's eye.

THE WASHINGTON MARCH

In early 1913 Alice Paul decided NAWSA should sponsor a national parade. Paul was the new chairman of NAWSA's Congressional Committee. It was based in Washington, D.C. The main purpose of the committee was to lobby Congress. Each year it asked lawmakers to support the Susan B. Anthony Amendment.

While studying in England Paul had joined a militant faction of the British suffrage movement. Its members defied laws and used violence. They were often jailed. Paul herself had been jailed several times. It was in a police station that she met another American, Lucy Burns. The two suffragists became good friends.

After Paul and Burns returned to the United States, they began working for NAWSA. The parade was their first planned event. Paul scheduled

ALICE PAUL (1885–1977)

Alice Stokes Paul was born in Moorestown, New Jersey, on January 11, 1885. She was raised as a Quaker. After graduating from Swarthmore College, she studied in England. There she became involved in the Women's Social and Political Union (WSPU). This militant suffrage group was led by Emmeline Pankhurst. Paul participated in demonstrations and spent time in jail. She drew on these experiences when she returned to the United States.

In 1913 Paul was appointed chairman of the Congressional Committee of NAWSA. That year, she and Lucy Burns founded the Congressional Union for Woman Suffrage. Paul served as president. The CU ultimately evolved into the National Woman's Party, founded in 1916. It became known for using tactics of nonviolent resistance and civil disobedience.

After the Nineteenth Amendment became part of the constitution, Paul went back to school. She earned several law degrees. But she also saw that obtaining the right to vote was only the beginning. Other battles for full citizenship and equality remained. Paul would seek to address those issues by proposing another amendment to the constitution. The Equal Rights Amendment was introduced in Congress in 1923. The amendment was eventually passed through Congress, but it was never ratified.

it for March 3, 1913. This was the day before the inauguration of President Woodrow Wilson. During the 1912 campaign Wilson had not taken a stand on suffrage. The suffragists hoped a national parade would convince the new president to support their cause.

The day of the parade was cold and sunny. An estimated 8,000 women formed seven separate marching divisions. In the front of one division rode a young woman on a white horse. Inez Milholland was a New York labor lawyer. She had appeared in New York City parades as a suffrage herald. And she had become a symbol of the women's movement.

LUCY BURNS (1879–1966)

Lucy Burns was born in Brooklyn, New York. She graduated from Vassar College. She later studied in Europe. In 1909, while at Oxford College in England, she became involved in the militant suffrage movement.

Upon her return to the United States, Burns worked for NAWSA. She and Alice Paul set up the first permanent suffrage headquarters in Washington, D.C. Their NAWSA committee lobbied the president and Congress to support a women's suffrage amendment. In 1914 Burns continued this work within the Congressional Union for Woman Suffrage (CU). She served as its vice chairman. The CU later became the National Woman's Party.

Burns headed the NWP's efforts to lobby Congress. During the 1914 and 1916 election campaigns, she organized CU efforts to defeat "the party in power." And she edited the NWP's weekly journal, *The Suffragist*.

Burns also led most of the NWP's White House demonstrations. She was arrested several times. One historian noted that Burns spent more time in prison than any other American suffragist. After passage of the Nineteenth Amendment, she retired from NWP work.

(Left) Suffragists line up for the March 1913 parade in Washington, D.C. Oregon had granted women the right to vote the previous year. (Right) The event's official program.

A few women wore costumes to represent ideals such as Liberty, Democracy, and Justice. Other women wore white dresses with yellow sashes that demanded "Votes for Women." Similar messages were carried on gold cloth banners and pennants. Golds and yellows predominated. They were the identifying colors of U.S. suffragists.

The marchers, 26 floats, and 10 bands made their way down Pennsylvania Avenue. In some places the crowds grew hostile. Some men jeered and spat at the women. Others blocked the way of the marchers. Women were pushed and hit. A few men tried to climb on the floats. The

FAST FACT

Suffragists first used gold and yellow for the prosuffrage cause in 1867. That is when Elizabeth Cady Stanton and Susan B. Anthony campaigned for the women's right to vote in Kansas. For their logo they used the Kansas state flower—the sunflower.

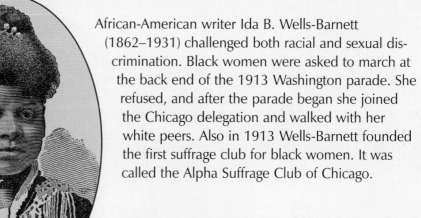

African-American writer Ida B. Wells-Barnett (1862–1931) challenged both racial and sexual discrimination. Black women were asked to march at the back end of the 1913 Washington parade. She refused, and after the parade began she joined the Chicago delegation and walked with her white peers. Also in 1913 Wells-Barnett founded the first suffrage club for black women. It was called the Alpha Suffrage Club of Chicago.

police did nothing to protect the women. And no arrests were made.

The following day newspapers reported what had happened. The police were criticized for failing to protect the women. Harriot Stanton Blatch sent a telegram to President Wilson. She said, "[Y]esterday the government, which is supposed to exist for the good of all, left women while passing in peaceful procession . . . at the mercy of a howling mob." A few days later, a congressional investigation was held.

Paul and Burns got what they wanted. The parade resulted in a lot of publicity. But they had only just begun.

THE CONGRESSIONAL UNION

Soon after, Paul and Burns founded a separate organization. It was called the Congressional Union for Woman Suffrage (CU). It assisted the work of NAWSA's Congressional Committee. But it was a separate organization. Paul was chairman of the Committee. And she served as president of the CU.

Many members of the Committee also belonged to the CU. Their work was the same, too. They handed out pamphlets. They held fundraisers. They sponsored petition drives. And they sent delegations to the president. They asked him to support a federal amendment. But Wilson would not.

Paul and NAWSA leaders began to have conflicts. They disagreed over finances. And they were at odds over tactics. NAWSA officials worried that Paul was too radical. That December, they demanded that she resign from the CU. She refused. In February 1914 NAWSA and Paul cut all ties.

The CU went on to establish itself as a separate suffrage organization. It began establishing state and local branches. That October it founded its own weekly journal. It was called *The Suffragist*.

Women and a child stand in front of the storefront office of the Congressional Union for Woman Suffrage branch in Colorado, 1914. Banners in the window read "Voting Women" and "Votes for Women."

In the spring of 1914, 5,000 women massed at the U.S. Capitol building in support of the women's suffrage amendment. Despite this impressive demonstration, Congress did not pass the amendment.

PROTESTING THE PARTY IN POWER

In March 1914 the U.S. Senate finally voted again on the women's suffrage amendment. The last time it had been considered was in 1887. During the vote more than a third of the senators abstained. To pass, the amendment needed 64 yes votes. It had only 35. And 34 opposed it.

That fall the CU announced a new policy. The group would hold "the party in power" responsible for not passing the federal amendment. The Democrats controlled the White House and Congress. So the CU would work against the Democrats in the midterm elections.

NAWSA leaders did not approve. They believed suffragists should be nonpartisan. They also worried about offending Democratic supporters. They denounced the CU for its militant approach. Paul defended the group, saying, "It is not militant in the sense that it means physical violence. It is militant only in the sense that it is strong, positive and energetic."

That energy attracted many members to the CU. They tended to be younger than NAWSA suffragists. They were also more likely to have college educations and career goals. Many CU members believed that strong action was needed to bring about change.

NINE STATES

In the fall of 1914, Congressional Union organizers traveled west. At that time women had gained full suffrage in nine states. All were in the western part of the United States.

The reason there were nine suffrage states was due to the efforts of NAWSA. State and local branches had continued to work to win suffrage. There had been little progress for several years. But a renewed effort in 1910 showed results. That year a suffrage referendum in Washington passed. Other states followed. California approved suffrage in 1911. Arizona, Kansas, and Oregon granted the right in 1912. And in 1913 the Territory of Alaska gave women the vote.

Some states allowed partial suffrage. In June 1913 the Illinois legislature gave women the right to vote in presidential and local elections.

FAST FACT

People who were against giving women the vote were called "antis." (The name came from the word *antisuffrage*.) In 1911 they formed the National Association Opposed to Woman Suffrage. It had 200,000 members. Its official journal was called *The Woman's Protest*.

A group of suffragists prepare to depart from the train station in Washington, D.C., to campaign for the vote in other states, 1914. Rose Winslow and Lucy Burns were headed to California; Doris Stevens and Ruth Astor Noyes were traveling to Colorado; Anna McGue was going to the state of Washington; and Jane Pincus and Jessie H. Stubbs were traveling to Arizona.

Illinois was the first state east of the Mississippi River to grant women the right to vote in a presidential election.

ELEVEN STATES

During the 1914 election campaign, CU suffragists spoke in support of a federal amendment. And they campaigned against all Democrats running for office.

But the strategy to oust Democrats from power did not work. And voters in North Dakota, South Dakota, Ohio, Missouri, and Nebraska all refused to allow women's suffrage. But referendums in Montana and Nevada succeeded. By the end of 1914, there were 11 suffrage states.

5

MODERATES AND MILITANTS

Suffragists had several defeats in 1915. That January the House of Representatives voted on the federal amendment for the first time. But it failed to pass. No state referendums passed at all. They were defeated in New Jersey, New York, Massachusetts, and Pennsylvania.

In San Francisco, Congressional Union volunteers set up a petition drive at the Panama Pacific Exposition. They gathered half a million names. That fall a convoy of cars carried the petition to Washington, D.C. A group of 2,000 women presented it to Congress. In December the suffrage amendment was again introduced in the Senate. But there was no vote.

NAWSA'S WINNING PLAN

At the end of 1915, Anna Howard Shaw stepped down as NAWSA president. Carrie Chapman Catt took her place.

Catt had worked hard to pass the New York referendum. And she was disappointed that it failed. As NAWSA president, she announced a new strategy. She called it the "winning plan." NAWSA would continue its disciplined effort to pass state referendums. When full suffrage seemed unlikely, the group would push for partial suffrage. At the same time,

Suffragists in Chicago hold signs encouraging people to vote against incumbent president Woodrow Wilson in the 1916 election. Alice Paul, leader of the National Woman's Party, believed that pressure from female voters in the few states where women were permitted to vote would force politicians to recognize the right of all American women to vote.

NAWSA would also lobby for a federal amendment. Lobbyists would work out of an office in Washington D.C. It was named Suffrage House.

THE NATIONAL WOMAN'S PARTY

In June 1916, the CU established an independent organization. Its first members were women who lived in suffrage states. Because most of these states were in the west, the new group was called the Woman's Party of Western Voters. Alice Martin served as chairman. The CU continued to work in states where women did not have the vote. Alice Paul remained its leader.

Within the year, the CU would merge with the Woman's Party. The resulting group would be known as the National Woman's Party (NWP).

WAITING FOR LIBERTY

In the fall of 1916, the CU continued its policy of opposing the party in power. Speakers traveled to suffrage states. They promoted passage of a federal amendment. And they campaigned against the Democrats.

Woodrow Wilson was running for re-election. War had broken out in Europe. But the United States had remained neutral. In 1916 Wilson campaigned with the slogan "Vote for Wilson, he kept us out of war." The activists' response was "Vote against Wilson, he kept us out of suffrage."

Inez Milholland Boissevain was with the CU campaign. In September 1916, she suddenly collapsed on a Los Angeles stage. She was ill with pernicious anemia, a serious blood disorder. She died 10 weeks later. The last words of her speech were, "President Wilson, how long must this go on—no liberty?"

That November Wilson was re-elected by a narrow majority. State referendums were defeated in Iowa, New Jersey, and West Virginia. But there was reason to celebrate. For the first time a woman would serve in the U.S.

Suffragist and lawyer Inez Milholland Boissevain (1886–1916) is pictured at a 1913 women's suffrage parade in New York City. Boissevain, who was just 31 years old when she died, became a martyr for the cause of women's rights. One NWP poster portrayed her as the activist "who died for the freedom of women."

Jeannette Rankin (1880–1973) delivers a speech at the office of the National American Woman Suffrage Association in 1917. Rankin, a Republican, served in the U.S. House of Representatives from 1917 to 1919. She later served a second term in the House from 1941 to 1943.

Congress. NAWSA lobbyist Jeannette Rankin of Montana was elected to the House of Representatives.

SUFFRAGE STUNTS

Suffragists continued to pressure the president. On December 2, 1916, one of the first U.S. female airplane pilots helped the New York Suffrage Association. Leda Richberg Hornsby flew over Staten Island, New York. She dropped suffrage pamphlets from her plane. Some leaflets fell on President Wilson's yacht. He was in the area for a ceremony at the Statue of Liberty.

A few days later, Wilson was back in Washington. He stood before Congress, delivering the State of the Union speech. Suddenly, six CU members flung a huge yellow banner from the gallery. They sat silently. But their sign demanded, "Mr. President, What Will You Do for Woman Suffrage?"

These actions got publicity. But many people disapproved of political protest. The acts were often dismissed as stunts.

PICKETING THE WHITE HOUSE

In early January 1917 a Woman's Party delegation met with Wilson. They presented him with resolutions to honor Boissevain. Then they asked him to give his support to the suffrage amendment. Wilson refused. And he abruptly left the meeting. NWP officials decided it was time to begin a new campaign. They would picket the White House.

At the time the NWP office was in Cameron House on Lafayette Square. The square bordered the White House. On the morning of January 10, Paul and 12 other women took a short walk to the president's home. They held two purple, white, and gold banners. One read, "Mr. President, What Will You Do for Woman Suffrage?" And the other rephrased Inez Milholland Boissevain's final words, "How Long Must Women Wait for Liberty?" At the gate of the White House, the women stood quietly. They held up the banners. And they said nothing. They spoke only in response to questions.

The "silent sentinels" appeared daily in front of the White House, picketing in hourly shifts. They were frequently organized according to their background. On some days, they represented their state. On other days, they represented their college or profession.

Women picket outside the White House, 1917.

The protests continued regardless of the weather. On bitterly cold days the women warmed their feet by standing on hot bricks. On stormy days they stood in pouring rain. It was both cold and rainy on March 4, the date of Wilson's second inauguration. That day 1,000 picketers ringed the White House. Every woman carried a banner. Some featured state insignias. Others carried slogans. The picketers' actions landed the issue of women's suffrage on the front page of almost every newspaper.

Wilson tolerated the protesters at first. But he had little sympathy for them. No group had ever used this political tactic before. Many people considered the women unpatriotic. And patriotism would soon be on everyone's mind. For on April 6 the United States entered World War I.

WORLD WAR I

Most NAWSA members were pacifists. But they accepted the government's decision to go to war. Catt declared that NAWSA would no longer agitate for the vote. Its members would help support the war. On April 10, she wrote, "Our Republic stands upon the threshold of what may prove the severest test of loyalty and endurance our country has ever had. It needs its women; and they are ready—as fearless, as willing, as able, as loyal as any women of the world."

NAWSA workers took on a variety of jobs. They did census work. They raised funds. And they sold war bonds. For their work, they were praised as patriots and citizens.

But Paul and her National Woman's Party were condemned. They continued to picket the White House. New signs asked how Wilson could fight

FAST FACT

Both NAWSA and the NWP adopted official colors. NAWSA's were blue and gold. The National Woman's party used purple, white, and gold.

for democracy overseas while denying it to women at home. One sign even referred to him as "Kaiser Wilson." NWP suffragists were accused of treason. They had banners torn from their hands. They were even attacked by angry mobs. But they continued to picket.

JAILED FOR FREEDOM

On June 22 six picketers were arrested. A week later eleven more were jailed for "obstructing traffic." Another group was arrested in mid-July. The arrested suffragists were fined $25. But they did not accept the charges. And they refused to pay. The protesters received sentences of up to six months.

The women served time in the Occoquan Workhouse in Virginia. They were not treated well. Their meals consisted of wormy cereals and soups. Some women received only bread and water. Meanwhile, more women joined the picket line.

A group of suffragists who had been arrested for picketing the White House leave the prison, 1918.

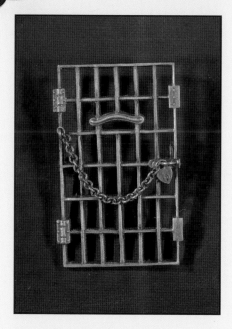

The National Woman's Party awarded a jailhouse door pin to members who went to prison in support of women's suffrage.

In October, with Congress preparing to recess, Paul left her organizing efforts. She joined the picketers and was arrested. In jail she, Lucy Burns, and several other women referred to themselves as political prisoners. They went on hunger strikes. Paul was committed to a psychiatric ward. She and other women were force-fed. Some were brutally beaten.

News of the women's treatment was smuggled to the outside. And newspapers gave it front-page coverage. Many people were upset. The United States was at war to protect democracy and freedom. Yet it was imprisoning its own citizens.

In response to the public outcry, the government began to release the picketers. By the end of November all of them had been set free. The following March a court declared the arrests invalid.

THE MODERATE APPROACH

NAWSA leaders did not approve of the NWP's militant tactics. Catt and Shaw believed the protests would cost the suffrage movement the goodwill of politicians. Catt worked to remain on good terms with President Wilson. NAWSA used a moderate approach in lobbying senators and representatives of the House. However, the civil disobedience of the NWP helped keep suffrage in the newspaper headlines.

In 1917 NAWSA celebrated more victories. In 1917 Arkansas passed a law giving women the right to vote in primaries. North Dakota, Nebraska, and Rhode Island gave women the right to vote for the president. And after a difficult campaign in New York, that state approved full suffrage for women.

6

THE NINETEENTH AMENDMENT

In early 1918 there were 12 full suffrage states. And there were 6 states with partial suffrage. This meant that more than 10 million women could vote in presidential elections. Almost 6 million were eligible to vote on all issues. In addition thousands of women were volunteering during the war. And another million had joined the workplace. These numbers helped President Woodrow Wilson change his mind.

For years Wilson had considered women's suffrage as an issue to be decided by the states. But on January 9, 1918, he released a written statement. He gave his full support to the suffrage amendment. The *New York Times* reported that Wilson believed its passage would be "as an act of right and justice to the women of the country and of the world."

A CLOSE VOTE

The following day the House of Representatives voted on the amendment. Several prosuffrage congressmen made sure they were present. Some left their sickbeds. Henry A. Barnhart of Indiana was carried in on a stretcher. Thetus W. Sims of Tennessee had broken his shoulder, but he refused to have it set. He did not want to miss the vote. Frederick C. Hicks, left his wife's deathbed in New York. She made him promise to vote in favor of suffrage.

FAST FACT

At its peak the National Woman's Party had 50,000 members. NAWSA was much larger. In 1919 it claimed more than 2 million members.

To pass, constitutional amendments must be approved by two-thirds of the House. The final vote was 274 in favor and 136 opposed. This was exactly the required two-thirds. It was now the Senate's turn.

A LOSS IN THE SENATE

Several months passed. Conservative senators managed to block any action until October. Meanwhile Wilson lobbied undecided senators to support the amendment. The day before the scheduled vote, he gave a speech before the Senate. He praised women for supporting the U.S. war effort. And he asked that they be rewarded. "We have made partners of women in this war," he said. They in return deserved "a partnership of privilege and right."

On October 1 the Senate voted. Outside the Capitol building NWP members picketed. Some were arrested. But the suffrage amendment also needed a two-thirds majority of the Senate. Of the 96 senators representing the 48 states, 62 voted in favor. But 64 votes were needed. Passage fell short by just two votes.

The mid-term elections that fall were busy. Suffragists campaigned hard in 1918 to support the election of prosuffrage politicians. The effort worked. Many suffrage supporters were elected. At the same time the party in power changed. Democrats lost seats in the Senate and House. And Republicans emerged with a greater majority in both legislative bodies. There were also two more full suffrage states. They were South Dakota and Oklahoma.

World War I ended in November. And NAWSA renewed agitation for the vote. Pressure also came from the international community. By the end of 1918, women in 19 countries had the right to vote. They included Australia, Canada, Russia, and Germany.

"WATCHFIRES FOR FREEDOM"

In December President Wilson left the country to participate in peace talks in Versailles, France. During the war he had spoken in defense of democracy. For its next protest the NWP called on Wilson to honor his words.

In early January 1919 NWP protesters set up an urn in front of the White House. In it they burned copies of Wilson's speeches that mentioned liberty and freedom. They called these protests "watchfires for freedom."

One of the "watchfire" demonstrations outside the White House, January 1919. Between 1917 and 1919 approximately 2,000 NWP suffragists picketed the White House. Of these, 168 women were arrested and jailed. Some of them returned to prison several times.

But it was against the law to have fires on public property. By the end of the month, dozens of women had been arrested. Paul was one of them. Rather than pay fines, they continued to choose to go to jail.

PASSAGE AND RATIFICATION

The following February the Senate voted again on the Susan B. Anthony Amendment. This time its passage fell short by just one vote.

On May 21, 1919, the House of Representatives again approved the amendment. This time, the favorable vote was by a wider margin. There

Sixty-sixth Congress of the United States of America;

At the First Session,

Begun and held at the City of Washington on Monday, the nineteenth day of May, one thousand nine hundred and nineteen.

JOINT RESOLUTION

Proposing an amendment to the Constitution extending the right of suffrage to women.

Resolved by the Senate and House of Representatives of the United States of America in Congress assembled (two-thirds of each House concurring therein), That the following article is proposed as an amendment to the Constitution, which shall be valid to all intents and purposes as part of the Constitution when ratified by the legislatures of three-fourths of the several States.

"ARTICLE ———.

"The right of citizens of the United States to vote shall not be denied or abridged by the United States or by any State on account of sex.

"Congress shall have power to enforce this article by appropriate legislation."

F. H. Gillett

Speaker of the House of Representatives.

Thos. R. Marshall

Vice President of the United States and President of the Senate.

The Nineteenth Amendment to the U.S. Constitution was passed by Congress on June 4, 1919. The Nineteenth Amendment became federal law when it was ratified on August 26, 1920. However, many southern states would not formally ratify the amendment for several decades. Mississippi did not ratify the amendment until 1984.

Women were often invited to watch state government officials sign the documents certifying ratification of the Nineteenth Amendment. This photo from January 1920 shows Kentucky governor Edwin P. Morrow signing the amendment, making Kentucky the 24th state to ratify.

were 304 "yes" votes and just 89 against. The following month the Senate voted again. And on June 4, 1919, the amendment was passed, 66 in favor to 30 opposed. The wording of the Nineteenth Amendment had remained unchanged since first introduced in 1878.

The next step was ratification. Three-fourths of the state legislatures had to approve the amendment. There were now 48 states in the country. To become part of the Constitution, the amendment had to be approved by 36 of them.

NAWSA and the NWP sent representatives across the nation. They urged state governors to call special sessions to bring the amendment before state legislators. And they lobbied legislators to vote for suffrage.

Wisconsin was the first to ratify. By mid-July, 11 states had given approval. That fall Carrie Chapman Catt spoke in 13 states in just eight weeks. Alice Paul campaigned in Maine. Their efforts to promote ratification worked. By the end of 1919, 22 states had ratified the Nineteenth Amendment.

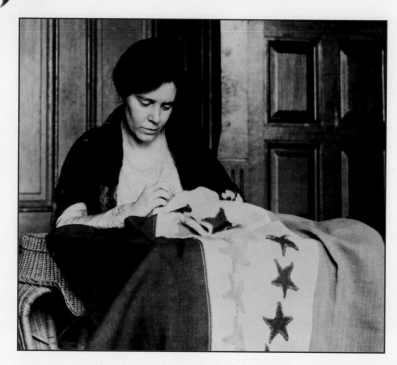

As each state ratified the amendment, Alice Paul stitched a star on a standard. In August 1920 she sewed the 36th and final star. She then unfurled the banner from the balcony of the NWP headquarters.

But several state legislatures refused to ratify. Most were in the South. Georgia and Alabama rejected the amendment in 1919. South Carolina, Virginia, Maryland, Mississippi, Delaware, and Louisiana defeated it in 1920. Still, by the end of March 1920, 35 states had approved the Nineteenth Amendment.

In June both political parties held their presidential conventions. The U.S. presidential elections would take place that fall. For the first time, both the Republican and Democratic Parties endorsed the amendment as part of their platform.

THE 36TH STATE

That August a special legislative session was held in Tennessee. Catt and other NAWSA leaders traveled to Nashville. They worked alongside local suffragists, including NWP members. Activists canvassed legislators, wrote letters, and made speeches. They realized that the fight for the women's

FAST FACT

In 1919 NAWSA reorganized. It became the League of Woman Voters. The group worked to encourage women to participate in the vote. It also worked on protective labor laws and educational issues.

vote could be decided by the Tennessee legislature. But suffrage opponents were also in Nashville. The liquor lobby and antisuffrage groups threatened a favorable vote.

The amendment easily passed in the Tennessee State Senate. But debate went on for three weeks in the House of Representatives. Finally, on August 18, the Tennessee House was called to a vote. One of the legislators was 24-year-old Harry Burn. He had initially voted against suffrage. But he received a letter from his mother. Febb Ensminger Burn made her wishes clear. "Hurrah, and vote for suffrage!" she wrote. So Harry Burn switched sides. And the amendment passed by a single vote. Tennessee became the 36th state to ratify the Nineteenth Amendment.

SUCCESS

More than 70 years had passed since the Seneca Falls Convention. And more than 50 years had gone by since the founding of the NWSA and the AWSA. Several generations of women activists had campaigned without a break for this moment. Women had run hundreds of campaigns. And they had finally succeeded.

On August 26, 1920, the U.S. secretary of state, Bainbridge Colby, issued the Nineteenth Amendment's proclamation. That day 27 million women gained full suffrage rights.

CHAPTER NOTES

p. 9: "Well I have been & gone . . ." Susan B. Anthony, quoted in Lynn Sherr, *Failure Is Impossible: Susan B. Anthony in Her Own Words* (New York: Random House, 2010), 110.

p. 10: "knowingly voting without having . . ." John D. Lawson, ed. *American State Trials: A Collection of the Important and Interesting Criminal Trials Which Have Taken Place in the United States*, Vol. 3 (St. Louis, Mo.: F. H. Thomas Law Book, 1915), 1.

p. 11: "it is the duty . . ." "Declaration of Sentiments," in Elizabeth Cady Stanton, Susan B. Anthony, Matilda Joslyn Gage, eds. *History of Woman Suffrage*, Vol. 1 (New York: Fowler & Wells, 1889), 72.

p. 11: "The right is ours . . ." Elizabeth Cady Stanton, in Ann D. Gordon, ed. *The Selected Papers of Elizabeth Cady Stanton and Susan B. Anthony*, Vol. 1 (Piscataway, N.J.: Rutgers University Press, 1997), 105.

p. 13: "all persons born or naturalized . . ." The Charters of Freedom: Constitution of the United States, Amendments 11–27. http://www.archives.gov/exhibits/charters/constitution_amendments_11-27.html

p. 14: "[I]n . . . voting, I not only . . ." Susan B. Anthony, quoted in William Safire, ed. *Lend Me Your Ears: Great Speeches in History* (New York: W. W. Norton, 2004), 694.

p. 14: "true and devoted . . . failure is impossible." Susan B. Anthony, quoted in Sherr, *Failure Is Impossible*, 324.

p. 15: "Men, their rights and nothing . . ." Helen Rappaport, *Encyclopedia of Women Social Reformers*, Vol. 1 (Santa Barbara, Calif.: ABC-CLIO, 2003), 20.

p. 17: "the full rights of . . ." Elizabeth Cady Stanton, in Ann D. Gordon, ed. *The Selected Papers of Elizabeth Cady Stanton and Susan B. Anthony*, Vol. 3 (Piscataway, N.J., 2003), 234.

p. 17: "The right of citizens . . ." The Charters of Freedom: Constitution of the United States, Amendments 11–27. http://www.archives.gov/exhibits/charters/constitution_amendments_11-27.html

p. 18: "There is scarce . . ." Elizabeth Cady Stanton, *Eighty Years and More (1815-1897): Reminiscences of Elizabeth Cady Stanton* (New York: European Publishing, 1898), 169.

p. 19: "Voice of the women's . . ." Carrie Chapman Catt, quoted in Alice Stone Blackwell, *Lucy Stone: Pioneer of Woman's Rights* (Charlottesville: University Press of Virginia, 2001), 240.

p. 22: "the chief work of suffragists . . ." Carrie Chapman Catt, quoted in Lee Ann Banazak, *Why Movements Succeed or Fail: Opportunity, Culture, and the Struggle for Woman Suffrage* (Princeton, N.J.: Princeton University Press, 1996), 48.

An office of the National American Woman Suffrage Association in Cleveland, 1912.

p. 25:   "Seeking no favors . . ." Mary Terrell, quoted in Christine Stansell, *The Feminist Promise: 1792 to the Present* (New York: Random House, 2010), 134.

p. 26:   "[T]he State is but the . . ." Elizabeth Boynton Harbert, quoted in Elizabeth Cady Stanton, Susan B. Anthony, Matilda Joslyn Gage, eds. *History of Woman Suffrage*, Vol. 3 (New York: Fowler & Wells, 1887), 78–79.

p. 34:   "[Y]esterday the government, which . . ." Harriot Blatch, quoted in Elizabeth Frost-Knappman, *Women's Suffrage in America: An Eyewitness History* (New York: Facts on File, 1992), 315.

p. 37:   "It is not militant . . ." Alice Paul, quoted in *Alice Paul and the American Suffrage Campaign* (Urbana: University of Illinois Press, 2007), 32.

p. 41:   "Vote for Wilson . . . out of suffrage," Deborah G. Felder, *A Century of Women: The Most Influential Events in Twentieth-Century Women's History* (Secaucus, N.J.: Citadel, 2003), 102.

p. 41:   ""President Wilson, how long . . ." Inez Milholland Boissevain, quoted in Linda Lumsden, *Inez: The Life and Times of Inez Milholland* (Bloomington: Indiana University Press, 2004), 174.

p. 43:   "How long must . . ." Mary Walton, *A Woman's Crusade: Alice Paul and the Battle for the Ballot* (New York: Palgrave Macmillan, 2010), 148.

p. 44:   "Our Republic Stands upon . . . " Carrie Chapman Catt, quoted in "Progressive Reform: Votes for Women." National Archives and Records Administration. http://www.archives.gov/exhibits/treasures_of_congress/text/page18_text.html

p. 47:   "as an act of right . . ." Woodrow Wilson, quoted in "Wilson Backs Amendment for Woman Suffrage," *New York Times*, January 10, 1918.

p. 48:   "We have made partners . . ." Frost and Cullen-DuPont, *Women's Suffrage in America*, 316.

p. 53:   "Hurrah, and vote . . ." quoted in Walton, *A Woman's Crusade: Alice Paul and the Battle for the Ballot*, 243.

CHRONOLOGY

1848: On July 19 and 20, the first women's rights convention is held in Seneca Falls, New York. Women publicly demand the right to vote.

1865: The Civil War ends in April. Elizabeth Cady Stanton and Susan B. Anthony begin a campaign for universal suffrage.

1867: Anthony founds the American Equal Rights Association, which works for universal suffrage. The first state suffrage referendum is defeated in Kansas.

1869: The suffrage movement splits. Stanton and Anthony found the National Woman Suffrage Association. Lucy Stone and others found the American Woman Suffrage Association. Wyoming Territory grants women's suffrage.

1872: Anthony is arrested for voting in Rochester, New York.

1875: In *Minor v. Happersett*, the U.S. Supreme Court determines that women are not eligible to vote.

1876: On July 4, in Philadelphia, Anthony disrupts Centennial celebrations by reading aloud "The Declaration for the Rights of Women."

1878: On January 10 the woman suffrage amendment, later called the Susan B. Anthony Amendment, is introduced in Congress.

1881: Stanton, Anthony, and Matilda Joslyn Gage publish the first volume of *History of Woman Suffrage*.

1887: On January 25 the U.S. Senate votes for the first time on the suffrage amendment. It is defeated.

1890: On February 18 the NWSA and the AWSA merge to form the National American Woman Suffrage Association (NAWSA). In July Wyoming becomes the first state to grant women the vote.

1900: Anthony retires as president of NAWSA. Carrie Chapman Catt is elected president.

1904: Anna Howard Shaw is elected NAWSA president.

1907: Harriot Stanton Blatch founds the Equality League of Self Supporting Women (later known as the Women's Political Union).

1910: The first women's suffrage parade takes place in New York City.

1913: Women's suffrage gains national attention after a NAWSA parade is held in Washington, D.C. Alice Paul and Lucy Burns found the Congressional Union for Woman Suffrage (CU).

1914: In February the CU breaks away from NAWSA. The following month the U.S. Senate defeats the woman suffrage amendment. During the fall election campaigns, the CU adopts the policy of protesting the party in power.

1915: In January the U.S. House rejects the suffrage amendment. In December Carrie Chapman Catt assumes presidency of NAWSA.

1916: The CU organizes the first woman's political party, the Woman's Party of Western Voters. In November Jeannette Rankin becomes the first woman elected to the House of Representatives.

1917: The Congressional Union and the Woman's Party of Western Voters unite. They form the Woman's National Party (WNP). In January NWP silent sentinels begin picketing the White House. On April 6 the United States enters World War I. In June arrests of NWP picketers begin.

1918: In January President Wilson publicly declares support for the suffrage amendment; it passes in the House of Representatives. In October, it fails in the Senate. On November 11, World War I ends.

1919: In May the House passes the suffrage amendment. In June the Senate passes it, and the ratification process begins.

1920: On August 18 the Nineteenth Amendment is ratified by the Tennessee House of Representatives. It becomes federal law on August 26.

GLOSSARY

amendment—a legal change to the U.S. Constitution.

electorate—the people in an area who are qualified to vote in an election.

lobby—to try to influence politicians or public officials about a particular issue.

militant—a radical; someone representing an extreme political view.

moderate—a person, organization, or political party that is not considered extreme or radical.

picketing—the practice of standing or walking at a specific location, usually with signs, to gain support for a cause.

ratify—to formally approve or make official.

referendum—a general vote by the electorate on a single political question.

suffrage—the right to vote.

suffragist—a reformer who worked during the 1800s and early 1900s to help women obtain the legal right to vote.

temperance—the practice of refraining from drinking alcohol.

FURTHER READING

FOR YOUNGER READERS

Burgan, Michael. *The 19th Amendment*. Minneapolis, Minn.: Compass Point Books, 2006.

Gourley, Catherine. *Gibson Girls and Suffragists: Perceptions of Women from 1900 to 1918*. Minneapolis, Minn.: Lerner Publishing, 2008.

Macdonald, Fiona. *You Wouldn't Want To Be a Suffragist!: A Protest Movement That's Rougher Than You Expected*. New York: Franklin Watts, 2009.

Rossi, Ann M. *Created Equal: Women Campaign for the Right to Vote, 1840–1920*. Washington D.C.: National Geographic, 2005.

Stone, Tanya Lee. *Elizabeth Leads the Way: Elizabeth Cady Stanton and the Right to Vote*. New York: Henry Holt, 2008.

FOR OLDER READERS

Baker, Jean H. *Sisters: The Lives of America's Suffragists*. New York: Hill & Wang, 2005.

Colman, Penny. *Elizabeth Cady Stanton and Susan B. Anthony: A Friendship That Changed the World*. New York: Henry Holt, 2011.

Walton, Mary. *A Woman's Crusade: Alice Paul and the Battle of the Ballot*. New York: Macmillan, 2010.

INTERNET RESOURCES

http://memory.loc.gov/ammem/collections/suffrage/nwp/

This Library of Congress American Memory site presents background information and photographs of protest efforts by members of the National Woman's Party. It links to images of imprisoned prisoners and essays with background information.

http://memory.loc.gov/ammem/vfwhtml/vfwhome.html

Suffrage pictures from 1850 to 1920 are featured on this American Memory website. It links to portraits of major figures and events of the women's suffrage movement. It also links to the timeline "One Hundred Years Toward Suffrage."

http://www.herstoryscrapbook.com/

The HerStory Scrapbook contains detailed information on the final four years of the women's suffrage campaign. Users navigate through a scrapbook of articles from the *New York Times* for the years 1917, 1918, 1919, and 1920. The site also includes information on important events in the history of women's suffrage.

http://www.pbs.org/stantonanthony/

The website for the film *Not for Ourselves Alone: The Story of Elizabeth Cady Stanton and Susan B. Anthony* provides biographical information on the two activists. It also features historical documents and essays on the women's movement.

INDEX

Numbers in **bold italics** refer to captions.

CONTRIBUTORS

LEEANNE GELLETLY is the author of several books for young adults, including biographies of Harriet Beecher Stowe, Mae Jemison, Roald Dahl, Ida Tarbell, and John Marshall.

Senior Consulting Editor **A. PAGE HARRINGTON** is executive director of the Sewall-Belmont House and Museum, on Capitol Hill in Washington, D.C. The Sewall-Belmont House celebrates women's progress toward equality—and explores the evolving role of women and their contributions to society—through educational programs, tours, exhibits, research, and publications.

The historic National Woman's Party (NWP), a leader in the campaign for equal rights and women's suffrage, owns, maintains, and interprets the Sewall-Belmont House and Museum. One of the premier women's history sites in the country, this National Historic Landmark houses an extensive collection of suffrage banners, archives, and artifacts documenting the continuing effort by women and men of all races, religions, and backgrounds to win voting rights and equality for women under the law.

The Sewall-Belmont House and Museum and the National Woman's Party are committed to preserving the legacy of Alice Paul, founder of the NWP and author of the Equal Rights Amendment, and telling the untold stories for the benefit of scholars, current and future generations of Americans, and all the world's citizens.